CANOEING

by Celeste A. Koon

HARVEY HOUSE, PUBLISHERS

NEW YORK, NEW YORK

ACKNOWLEDGEMENTS

This book was made possible by the generous help and assistance of the following people.

Mr. Robert Lantz of The Blue Hole Canoe Company
Mr. Roger McGregor of Alumacraft Boat Company
Mr. Dennis Phillips of Coleman Company, Inc.
Mr. John Gunner Berg of Great Canadian Canoe
The Public Archives of Canada
Mary Koon
Richard Orr
Bruce Norman

In addition, special thanks go to the canoeists featured on these pages.

Mary Bell   Alan Lambert
Bruce Brandes   Cheryl Lutz
Julie Burlbaw   Steven Picker
Dena Garton   Bruce White
Meg Gentry

And finally, for unsurpassed patience and assistance, I wish to thank my husband, Richard Koon.

Copyright©1982 by Celeste Koon
All rights reserved
Library of Congress Catalog Number: 80-84812
ISBN 0-8178-0019-0
Published in Canada by Fitzhenry & Whiteside, Ltd., Toronto
HARVEY HOUSE, Publishers, New York City, New York

CANOEING

CHAPTER ONE

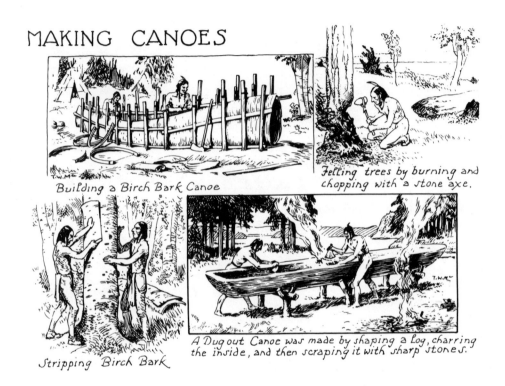

MAKING CANOES

Building a Birch Bark Canoe

Felling trees by burning and chopping with a stone axe.

Stripping Birch Bark

A Dug out Canoe was made by shaping a log, charring the inside, and then scraping it with sharp stones.

Public Archives of Canada photo number C-70275. Original drawing by C.W. Jeffreys.

There are those who say other kinds of transportation are better and faster than canoes. They may be right.

On the other hand, who floats rivers on a skateboard? Or fishes on horseback? Or runs rapids on a bicycle?

There are some places only a skinny canoe can take you. There are some adventures only a swift canoe can bring you. There are some secrets only a quiet canoe can teach you. Travel in a canoe has its advantages.

Canoeing is fun too. You can sleep under the stars as you camp on a creek. You can take pictures of diamonds on the water or your friends Marathon in Montana.

You can load your boat with tons of food and pole to hidden pools. You can laugh like a pirate as you sail in a salty breeze. As for fishing — canoeing and fishing go together like peanut butter and jelly!

A canoe is more than just transportation. Life in a canoe is more than just riding on water. Canoeing is all kinds of fun!

LONG-AGO CANOEISTS

Canoes, of course, are a very old way of getting around. The first canoes were made from hollowed-out logs. Dugout canoes were used by people all around the world.

People did amazing things in these simple boats. The ancient Polynesians traveled on thousand-mile trips in their huge double canoes. They used their canoes to discover many islands in the Pacific and to settle them.

Other ancient people carried on trade with their neighbors by canoe. And, most importantly, canoes have always been used for hunting and fishing. These small boats have helped the human race survive.

THE VOYAGEURS

In North America, the dugout boat underwent a big improvement. Indians began to make the canoe out of birch bark. Birch bark canoes had many advantages. For one thing, they were light enough to carry over rough places.

The Indians also improved the design. They made the sides of their birch bark canoes high so water wouldn't slop inside. They made the ends curve upwards so the canoe handled better.

The Indian canoe was so practical that the first white men were quick to see its value. The early French traders and trappers adopted the native canoe for their travel. The French traders, or **voyageurs**, as they were called, soon had the Indians build bigger canoes for them. Some of these canoes were almost 40 feet (12 m.) long and could carry 5,000 pounds (230 kg.). Yet, the boats themselves — built without nails or metal — weighed only about 300 pounds (130 kg.)!

A crew of fourteen men transported the canoe and its cargo over hundreds of miles. Smaller boats had a crew of eight.

These **voyageurs** led a rugged life. They paddled in rain or sun, and slept on the ground. They rarely took baths, and ate the same food all the time. Every day they had to paddle their huge canoe for 50 miles (80 km.)!

PRESENT DAY CANOEISTS

Today canoes are used more for recreation than work. Canoeing takes people away from their everyday chores — school work, jobs or housework. It's also a way to challenge your mental and physical abilities. The water does not always make a canoe trip easy. So when you get down the river or across the lake safely, you feel great! You have met the water's challenge.

Public Archives of Canada photo number C-2774. Painting by Mrs. F.A. Hopkins.

CHAPTER TWO

Few — if any — people are "natural" canoeists. To be a good canoeist, you have to know a lot. You have to know how to handle yourself and your boat in the water. You have to know how to care for your equipment, and what to wear. You have to gain experience knowing when and where to canoe. Fortunately, all these things can be learned. "River rats" are made, not born!

The first step in becoming a real river rat is to learn to swim. Nonswimmers should not go canoeing. A canoeist who can't swim is like a baseball player who can't hit. Would you want this person on your team? Would you want a canoeing partner who won't know what to do if he gets wet? Learning to swim is one of the basic skills that goes with this sport.

CANOE CLASSES

The next step is to take some kind of lessons in canoeing. The YMCA or city parks department sometimes offers classes in canoeing. Or you may be able to learn through a Scout or Red Cross course.

If you can't find a class, a qualified adult can teach you. You can ask the YMCA, parks department, Scout or Red Cross office to recommend someone.

A third way to learn is to join a canoeing or whitewater club. To find out about a club in your area, ask at a store that sells canoes. Or write to The American Canoe Association, Box 248, Lorton, Va. 22079. They will send you a list of clubs in your area.

The American Canoe Association, American Whitewater Affiliation and The United States Canoeing Association each have a magazine. You can get it free by joining or you might be able to borrow someone else's copy. Try the library for books and magazines, too.

With someone to coach you, learning to canoe is not too hard. But learning to canoe without help is like learning to play baseball by watching a game on TV with the sound off!

Photo courtesy of the Coleman Company, Inc.

"River rats" on the Niangua River in Missouri.

GET IN SHAPE

Canoeing flexes some muscles that most of us don't use very often. So unless you are a shot-putter or a house painter, you may want to get in shape. Here are some exercises you can do to strengthen those important back, shoulder and arm muscles.

1. Hold your arm straight out in front of you. Squeeze a tennis ball and turn your wrist back and forth at the same time. Repeat with the other arm. Gradually increase the number of times you squeeze the ball.

2. Put your arms at your side. Hold a medium heavy rock in each hand (or a book), and raise your arms until they are straight out from the shoulder. Do this several times holding the rock downward, and several times with the rock resting on the palm of your hand.

3. Do some push ups.

4. Lie on the floor on your stomach. Put your arms straight out over your head. Now lift your arms and legs off the floor at the same time. Repeat.

5. Get in a crawling position. First, let your back sag. then arch it as high as you can. Repeat.

WHAT TO WEAR

Use common sense when you pack your bag for a canoe trip. Take comfortable clothes that you can get dirty. Dress for the weather you expect.

In summer, you will probably want to wear your swim suit or shorts. Take along a long-sleeved shirt and a towel. Sunlight reflecting off the water can give you a bad sunburn. You may need to cover your knees and shoulders to keep them from looking like stewed tomatoes.

Tennis shoes are a good choice. Special canvas river shoes are nice, but not necessary. Wearing tennis footlets (the kind with the ball on the back) will help keep rocks out of your shoes if you end up wading.

Don't forget insect repellent, suntan lotion, a hat and sunglasses. If you wear prescription glasses, use a headstrap. Glasses are too expensive to lose.

In winter, you have to be a lot more careful about what you wear. It's dangerous to be wet or cold while canoeing in winter. Be sure you wear plenty of clothes, and take extras. Wool or synthetic pile clothing is best. These fabrics can help keep you warm even if they're wet.

There are several ways to keep your extra clothes dry. You can put them in special plastic canoe bags. These bags are sold at canoe stores and they work very well.

A cheaper method is to put your clothes inside two garbage bags and tie the garbage bags inside a nylon duffel bag and strap it to the canoe. You can buy nylon duffel bags at Army Surplus stores.

Plastic pickle barrels that restaurants have also make good waterproof containers. One disadvantage is that it takes longer to get in and out of them, but you can usually get them free from a restaurant that serves hamburgers. Just make sure the lid snaps tight.

Pay attention to the weather, and dress so you will be comfortable on a canoe trip.

Finally, wear a wetsuit whenever you float a river with really cold water, and always take extra care when you get wet and cold. If you can't stop shivering, change your clothes or build a fire. Getting chilled to the bone at any time of the year can bring on a serious condition called hypothermia. More about hypothermia is explained on page 63.

One good way to learn how to canoe is to join a canoeing or whitewater club. Such clubs often hold clinics and lessons for beginners, and take group floats. Photo courtesy of The Blue Hole Canoe Company.

WHEN TO GO

As long as the water isn't frozen, you can have fun canoeing. Each season has its special charm. Spring brings wildflowers and better floating conditions. Summertime is a great time for splashing and fishing. Autumn means crisp days and colorful leaves. Winter is ideal for seeing wildlife and finding peace on the river.

WHERE TO GO

Find some water! With the right preparations and weather, canoes can float safely in oceans, lakes, rivers, ponds and swamps. Take your pick. Once you have chosen your route, use the following checklist to finish your preparations. The letters will help you remember there are five things you should check before you put in.

C   CHARTS AND MAPS
Do you have charts or maps of where you plan to go? You will need a map in case of emergency, or if you get lost.

A   ASK AROUND
Have you asked someone about river conditions today? Even if you have floated the river before, ask the outfitter, ranger or other local person about the water conditions. They can warn you about any new hazards.

N   NOTES
Did you leave a note with someone telling where you are going and when you'll be back? People won't come looking for you unless they know you are missing.

O   OTHERS

Do you have an adult and at least one other canoe along with you? Three canoes are even better. If an emergency arises, you will have more people to help.

E   ETIQUETTE

Do all the people in your party know basic river etiquette? Don't litter. Don't go to the bathroom within 100 feet of the water. Don't throw burnt logs in the river, or wash dishes there. The idea behind river etiquette is to leave the stream or lake as nice (or nicer) than you found it.

Finally, there are a few places you should not canoe. Do not trespass on private land. Respect all posted areas. Check before you float on the property of military installations. Pay attention to the warnings of local people, park rangers or the Coast Guard. Believe them if they say it's not safe to float.

MAPS

One way to find maps is to visit the library and check out a book on canoeing that has a good chapter on where to go. A good book which is all about how to locate maps and outfitters is **Canoeing and Rafting** by Sara Pyle. This book, and others like it, have pages and pages of addresses. It also tells whether the maps are free or not.

Another way to get maps is to turn to the words "United States" in the phone book. The U.S. Forest Service and the U.S. Department of Agriculture can be of great help. Write or call them for information.

Your state's parks department, conservation department, tourism department or fish and game department will have maps and information too. You shouldn't have much trouble getting maps or finding places to float. After all, the earth has more water than land!

CHAPTER THREE

By the time you read this book, canoe equipment will cost more. So use the prices listed here as a guide. They show which items have cost the most in the past. Call a canoe store to find out what they cost now.

LIFE JACKETS

The single most important item you need is a life jacket. Can you make it safely down the river without a life jacket? Maybe. But what if you turn over in cold water? Few people last long in really cold water. And what if you hit your head on a rock? It's hard to swim while you're unconscious.

Your life jacket is life insurance. Get one and wear it!

When you look for a life jacket, make sure you get one that is Coast Guard approved. Get one that fits. Don't get a life jacket that's two sizes too big and plan to grow into it. It might come off accidentally. One that is too small is just as bad. It might not keep you high enough out of the water. Read the label to find out how many pounds the life jacket will support.

There are two kinds of jackets that are approved for use on canoes. The least expensive is the familar orange stuffed-collar type. They cost about $5, are quite safe when worn properly, but they may not last as long as some of the other kinds. Too, these collar-type life jackets are not suitable for white-water canoeing.

If you know that you want to take up whitewater canoeing sometime, you may want to get a life jacket which would be allowed in whitewater competitions. They look like vests, contain foam inside a nylon cover and use a zipper instead of rings and straps. The best ones also have a waist belt and a movable flap over the hips that lets you sit down more easily. These jackets cost about $30 to $45.

Do not get a ski belt. These are not suitable for canoeing. If you take a boat cushion along, use it as an extra device, not as a substitute for a life jacket.

HELMETS

Helmets are not necessary on gentle rivers or flat water, but if you paddle in whitewater — especially rock-strewn whitewater — a helmet is a must. Helmets come in plastic or fiberglass, and cost about $20 to $30. They look like ice hockey helmets.

CANOES

There are several hundred models of canoes, more than anybody can memorize. However, by learning what to look for, you can tell what kind of water a canoe is designed for. Study a canoe very carefully if you intend to buy it.

First, look and see if the canoe is decked or open. Open canoes — those without a spray skirt or molded cover on top — are called cruising or touring canoes. They perform best on lakes or streams without heavy whitewater.

The top photo shows a decked canoe and the bottom picture shows an open canoe. Photos courtesy of Great Canadian Canoe Company.

Decked canoes are made for whitewater and racing. A kayak is technically a decked canoe. You can tell whether a decked boat is for one or two persons by the number of cockpits.

Next, find out the length of the canoe. Canoes 15 feet or less are usually paddled by one person. Sixteen- and 17-foot canoes are commonly used for two people, while 18-foot canoes can carry three people, or two people with a lot of gear. Canoes longer than 18 feet are mainly used at summer camps.

You should also check the width of the canoe at the middle of the boat, and the general shape of the canoe. Canoes made for cruising and carrying gear are wider, and flatter on the bottom. They have a "U" or horseshoe shape. Canoes made for racing are usually narrower and have a steeper, more "V"-looking hull.

You can tell which end is the stern (back) and which is the bow (front) by glancing at the seats. See where the leg room is. It would be nearly impossible to sit on the stern seat backward!

A canoe with a square stern end is designed for an outboard motor. If the canoe is a "double ender," that is, if both ends are pointed, any motor would have to be side-mounted.

Look at the keel. Is there a keel? Is the keel almost flat? This is called a shoe keel. Flat keels and canoes without keels perform better in fast water. If the keel hangs down about an inch (2½ cm.) the canoe is made for navigating on a lake.

The last thing you want to know — but not the least — is what the canoe is made from. Few wooden or wood-and-canvas canoes exist today, but some wood-canvas-plastic canoes are made. Most modern canoes are made from aluminum, fiberglass, ABS plastic or Kevlar.

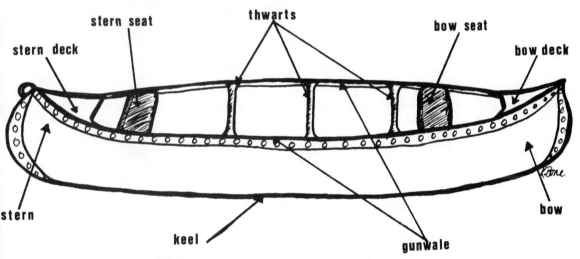

Drawing by Kim Bone.

Aluminum canoes have several advantages. They are durable, they don't require special maintenance and they cost less than most other kinds of canoes. A good, tempered aluminum canoe costs about $400 to $500. A tempered canoe has been heat-treated to make the aluminum extra-strong. An aluminum canoe which is not tempered will cost less, but probably not last as long. Among the disadvantages, aluminum canoes are noisy, dent easily, and they are hard to repair.

A good fiberglass boat costs about $400 to $600. Fiberglass won't dent, and it's easily repaired, but it's hard to tell a good fiberglass boat from a bad one. Stick to well-known firms when buying a fiberglass canoe. Cheap fiberglass canoes may handle poorly, as well as break in half.

ABS is a plastic often sandwiched between foam and vinyl. Some ABS plastics have trade names such as Royalex or Oltonar. This material has a "memory." Amazingly enough, dents and bulges return to their original shape. Some of these canoes have been dropped from a five-story building without harm! ABS canoes cost about $600 to $800. Again, it is a good idea to buy from a well-known company since the ABS is covered by vinyl and you can't see it.

Kevlar combines strength with lightness and is one of the newest materials used in canoe building. It is also quite expensive. A Kevlar canoe costs about $900 to $1,200.

You can buy a used canoe. Take a person with you who knows how canoes are built. Check for punctures, bent or broken ribs and a straight keel. The age of a used canoe is not as important as its condition.

If you don't want to buy a canoe, you can always rent one. Renting a canoe usually costs about $8 to $15 a day. If you need transportation, the outfitter will put you and your canoe on the river, or pick you up. The fee depends on the distance you float and the number of canoes.

To find an outfitter, write the chamber of commerce in a town near where you plan to float, or write that state's department of tourism. Sporting goods stores often have pamphlets with rates from different outfitters. In popular areas, you may want to call ahead and make a reservation.

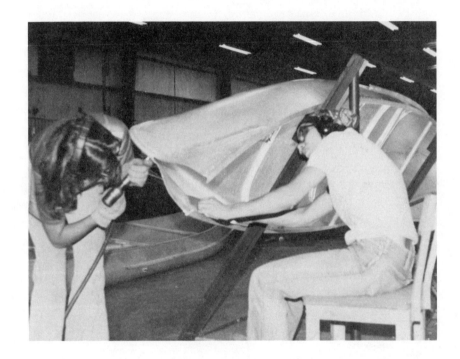

An aluminum canoe being made. Photo courtesy of Alumacraft Boat Company.

(Top left) A Royalex canoe comes to grief on the St. Francis River in Missouri.

(Bottom left) The same Royalex canoe is hauled out of the St. Francis.

(Above) The same Royalex canoe returns to the river. Photos courtesy of The Blue Hole Canoe Company.

PADDLES

There are many different kinds of paddles. Paddles can be made of wood, plastic, fiberglass or combinations of these materials. Standard canoe paddles cost $10 to $30, although paddles in special styles or materials may cost as much as $60.

The best way to select a paddle is to try a few out. The right paddle should be long enough so you can dip the whole blade in the water as you stroke without leaning sideways. And it should be short enough so your hand does not rise above eye level at the beginning of a stroke. Another handy, but less accurate, method of choosing a paddle is to pick one that comes to your chin.

Take good care of your paddle and it will last longer. Don't use it as a pole if you can help it. Mend little cracks or splits as soon as they appear. Put a wet wooden paddle in the shade so the sun doesn't warp it. Stand your paddle against a tree so nobody steps on it.

Finally, it's a good idea to take an extra paddle along for each person. If one gets lost or broken, you won't have to paddle with your hands!

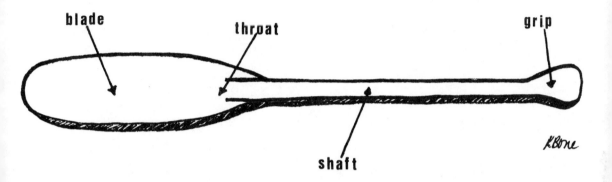

blade   throat   grip

shaft

Drawing by Kim Bone.

OTHER EQUIPMENT

A well-prepared canoeist takes a few other items on a trip. These items include at least 30 feet of rope, a first aid kit, duct tape and maybe kneepads.

Cut the rope in half, and attach one piece to each end of the canoe. Coil the rope loosely on the floor while floating. In case the canoe turns over, the rope will fall out, making it easier to grab the canoe as it floats out of reach. You can also untie the rope if a rescue is necessary.

Silver duct tape that you buy at hardware stores has saved many a canoeist from a long walk! It keeps on sticking even when it's wet. Use duct tape to make a temporary patch in your canoe. It's a lot better than trying to bail and paddle at the same time.

You should always take a first aid kit with you on a canoe trip. You never know when you'll need a bandaid — or worse. Useful items for a first aid kit include:

Bandaids	Baking soda
Sterile patches	Cotton balls
Gauze wraps	Aspirin
An elastic bandage	Adhesive tape
Bactine or first aid cream	Water purification tablets
Alka Seltzer	Daily medicine you must take
Needle, thread and safety pins	

Small items like cotton balls or baking soda can be stored in plastic film containers. Your whole first aid kit can be put in a coffee can with a lid, a Tupperware box, an old tackle box or inside two Ziplock bags.

After that, place your first aid kit in a duffel bag or a plastic bag that's tied to the canoe. Another trick is to take an old pair of panty hose and put one leg inside the other. Then stuff your first aid kit down inside the legs and tie the hose securely to the canoe. Your first aid kit is no good at the bottom of the lake!

Kneepads are useful if you plan to do a lot of whitewater canoeing. Basketball kneepads are about $5, and real whitewater kneepads are about $20.

Many other accessories are available for canoes. Visit a sporting goods store or a specialty canoe shop to learn about car-top carriers, sailing rigs, outboard motors or folding seats.

Inexperienced canoeists on the Current River, a National Scenic Riverway in Missouri.

CHAPTER FOUR

Once in a while, you will see people zigzagging their way down a river. They could be chasing turtles. They could be swatting mosquitos. But most of the time they don't know how to paddle. So ZIG, they hit a rock! Or ZAG, they turn over on a limb in the water.

By learning the different strokes, you can prevent things like this from happening to you. If you know the right way to paddle, you won't be nearly as likely to lose your glasses, your matches and hot dogs, the soda — or your mind!

GETTING PERFECT

Take lessons, or practice the strokes on a small lake before you leave home. If you can't do that, practice at the first quiet pool you find on a river. Make sure a qualified adult is around. Wear your life jacket.

LAUNCHING AND LOADING

The bottom of your canoe will get plenty of scrapes and dents by accident. So when you launch, you want to keep the hull from scraping across the rocks.

To launch, two people should carry the canoe to the edge of the water. One person should stand on each side near the middle of the boat. Next, lower the bow (front) end until it touches the water. Then, hand over hand, slide the rest of the canoe out from shore.

If you have things to load in the canoe, you may want to turn the boat so one long side of it is right by the shore. This makes it easier to reach.

To load correctly, put the heaviest items a little closer to the stern (back) than the bow. Make sure heavy items sit squarely in the center of the floor, or place two heavy things side by side. Stow the lightest gear on top.

Stuff anything that should stay dry inside garbage bags, canoe bags or plastic barrels. Tie all your gear to the canoe unless it is so heavy it would make the canoe too hard to rescue if you swamped.

A properly loaded canoe should ride slightly higher in the front than in the back. The load should be distributed so the canoe doesn't lean more to one side than the other. Your canoe will feel tippy and handle poorly if it's not loaded right.

Always take a plastic bag for trash with you. Never leave it open while you ride. If you spill, it does too. A clean waterway is the responsibility of every canoeist.

BOARDING

You don't want to turn the canoe over just getting in. This is funny for other people to watch, but your partner may never speak to you again! So put the paddles in the canoe, fasten your life jacket, and have the person who is going to sit in the stern hold the canoe between their knees.

Next, the person who is going to sit in the bow should climb carefully to the seat. Bend over and hold onto the gunwales (sides) as you go. Keep your feet near the center of the canoe.

Once the bow person has the paddle ready, the stern person gives a slight push and hops in. This works most of the time. On occasion, however, you might have to launch in water that is two inches deep. Then at least one person will have to get out and wade until the canoe reaches deeper water.

A properly loaded canoe should ride slightly higher in the front than in the back. The load should be stable. Photo courtesy of The Blue Hole Canoe Company.

HOLDING THE PADDLE

Place one hand over the top of the paddle as shown in the picture. Put the other hand around the neck near the blade. Try changing sides by reversing your hands. It's easy. Most canoe strokes are with a little practice.

This picture shows the correct way to hold the paddle.

BOW STROKE

The bow stroke is used to pull the canoe through the water. Reach out in front of you and dip the paddle in the water. Then sweep the blade through the water close to the canoe. Keep the blade turned so the wide face of the paddle pushes the water.

When the blade comes out of the water, about at your hip, turn your wrist so the paddle lies flat above the water. Keeping the blade flat, place the paddle out in front of you again. This is called feathering. Now you are in position to do the stroke again.

BACKPADDLE

The backpaddle is an important stroke — especially for whitewater canoeists. The backpaddle stroke slows the canoe in fast water, giving you more time to size up a situation. In a sluggish current, the backpaddle should bring you to a stop.

The backpaddle is the reverse of the bow stroke. Swing the paddle back and dip it in the water behind you. Sweep the wide part of the blade through the water toward the front of the canoe. As the blade comes out of the water, feather the paddle backward past your hip again. Then start the stroke over.

J STROKE

The J stroke is another stroke which pulls the canoe through the water. At the same time, it helps steer the canoe.

The J stroke begins just like the bow stroke. Put the paddle out in front of you and sweep the blade through the water. When the blade gets past your hip, twist the paddle outward in a slight "J" shape. Slice the paddle out of the water once the face of the blade is parallel to the canoe.

The J stroke is mainly used by the stern person to keep the canoe on a straight course.

DRAW

The draw stroke is used to set the canoe over sideways — a very useful stroke when a rock is dead ahead. Reach your paddle straight out past your hip and dip it in the water. Pull the wide part of the blade toward you. Right before the blade hits the canoe, slice the paddle out of the water. The canoe will move toward the place where you first stuck the paddle in the water.

If two people draw stroke on the same side of the canoe, they should both be careful not to lean too far out. If two people draw stroke on opposite sides of the canoe, the canoe will turn around in a circle.

PUSH

The push is the opposite of the draw. It's not as easy or as efficient as the draw, but it can be used if you need to set the canoe over sideways and you don't have time to change sides for a draw stroke.

Stick the paddle in the water at your side. Push the wide part of the blade straight out as far as you can reach. Feather the paddle back and start over. The canoe will move sideways away from the direction you are pushing.

SWEEPS

Sweep strokes are used to turn the canoe. Often the bow person will turn the canoe with a full sweep or a half sweep. In a full sweep, the paddle is dipped into the water with the blade nearly parallel to the canoe. Then the paddle is swept in a big half circle away from the boat and back again.

A half sweep ends when one quarter of a circle is completed, and for this reason, this stroke is sometimes called a quarter sweep.

Sweeps can be reversed by beginning the stroke in back of you and sweeping in a half circle toward the bow (front) of the canoe. When one person sweeps on one side of the boat, and the other person reverse sweeps on the opposite side of the boat, the canoe will turn around in a small area.

ADVANCED STROKES

Once you have some experience, you may want to learn some advanced strokes such as the bow rudder, the pry, different braces and the Eskimo roll. These are more complicated, and you should have a qualified person teach you.

LANDING

It's usually easiest and best to land with the bow pointed upstream — especially in fast water. To turn upstream as you near the shore, one person should sweep on one side while the other person reverse sweeps on the opposite side.

Once you are out of the current, try to ease up gently on the shore. Then the person whose end is touching — usually the bow — should get out and steady the canoe between their knees. After that, the second person climbs out, keeping low as when boarding.

You can launch bow first when you are ready to leave if the water is not too swift. But many times you will want to turn the canoe around before you launch again.

Finally, remember to pull your canoe well up on shore. Otherwise, it might float off and leave you in the middle of the wilderness without any peanut butter and jelly!

Upon landing, the bow person should stay and steady the canoe while the stern paddler climbs out.

CHAPTER FIVE

Lakes are sometimes called "flat water." This means the water doesn't run downhill like water in a river. It doesn't mean the surface of the lake is really flat! In fact, lake canoeing often presents quite a challenge to the canoeist. Bad weather can toss a 17-foot canoe on a lake like a leaf on the ocean!

When you go lake canoeing, make sure an experienced adult goes along. Travel with more than one canoe. Try to learn the effect of weather, waves and wind on your canoe. It's to your advantage to be able to tell which of these forces will work against you, and which ones will help you.

WIND

A strong wind is the usual cause of whitecaps on a lake. Wind-driven waves can be more hazardous than they look. In a very strong wind it's usually wise not to travel. The waves will be higher in the middle of the lake than near the shore. A heavily loaded canoe can take on water in high waves. Or you might swamp if you get turned broadside.

On the other hand, a **moderate** wind is fine for traveling. When you travel in the same direction as a moderate breeze, the wind will help push your canoe and save you time and energy.

Even if you want to go into the wind, you can usually make progress against a medium breeze. First, you can tack. Tacking is zigzagging into the wind. You will paddle farther, but you will probably get there sooner than if you attempt to paddle straight ahead.

To tack, steer the canoe so it crests each wave at a slight angle. Paddle for a distance while you angle the canoe slightly to the right. Then paddle for a while, angling the canoe a little to the left. By doing this, you should be able to zigzag your way across the lake.

Another way to make progress against a bad wind is to head for the lee side of an island or shoreline. The side of an island or boat which faces the wind is called the windward side. The side that is sheltered from the wind is called the lee side. By traveling on the lee side of the land, you can avoid the worst effects of the wind.

WAVES

Besides the wind, several other factors cause wave action. Islands, the shape of the shoreline, and the depth of the lake all help make waves. These features can help and hinder you at the same time.

For example, islands can protect you from rough seas. But they can also prevent you from steering a direct course, and being able to see where you are going. Similarly, a shallow channel may have shallower waves — but with more cross currents. A shoreline with many coves can give you good places to fish, only it may take longer to follow all those curves.

So think ahead when you plan your route. Few lakes are as calm as a saucerful of water. Try to use the forces of nature to make your canoe trip more fun and less work.

WEATHER

Storms can lead to trouble. Stay alert and try to figure out what the weather will be. A portable radio, a cloud chart and a small book on the weather can all help you with the forecast. Old-time weather sayings may hold other clues. Many of them have been around for years because they're accurate. They are generally used to predict the weather for the next 12 hours.

One of the most practical sayings is about dew:

"When the grass is dry at morning light,
Look for rain before the night.
When the grass is dry at night,
Look for rain before the light."

Another rhyme which is usually accurate is:

"Red sky at night, sailor's delight;
Red sky at morning, sailor's warning."

Get the weather forecast, or check natural weather signs before you put in on flat water. Stay alert for changes in the weather.

ACROSS CHOPPY WATERS

If worse comes to worst, and an unexpected storm blows up, try to find shelter. Get to shore as soon as you see the storm coming. Don't wait for the storm to catch up with you. Wind-driven waves and lightning are both dangerous.

Suppose, though, you do get caught in the storm. Kneel down rather than sit. Keep your boat pointed directly into, or away from, the wind. Don't get broadside to the waves!

You can rig a sea anchor by tying 20 or 30 feet of rope to a bucket or cooking kettle. Then tie the rope to the stern. The kettle will drag in the water and help keep the canoe from turning sideways.

ACROSS FRIENDLY WATERS

The day dawns sunny and bright. Dewdrops glisten on your canoe, and the smell of bacon frying fills the air. It's a gorgeous day, just perfect for canoeing! All you have to do now is get where you are going.

First, mark the day's route on your map, or on a piece of paper. Then look out across the water in front of you. Figure out the direction you intend to go. Do you see any features in the landscape that match features on the map?

To paddle in a straight line, pick one feature as a landmark. Pick an island, a tall tree, a stream on shore, or something similar. Decide how far away from shore you should be when you pass this landmark. Then paddle right on the course you have sighted until you are even with the landmark. Once there, pick a new marker in the line you want to go. Then steer toward it.

Another way to keep yourself on course is to use a compass. Have someone teach you how to read the compass before you set out. A boat compass is better than a regular compass because a regular compass has to be held still to find north. A boat compass is also more expensive and needs to be mounted on a bracket.

Finally, check your map as you go along. Make sure you know where you are on the map as you pass each landmark. If you are not sure where you are, stop and find out. Binoculars are a big help in locating features along the shoreline, such as a stream entering the lake.

Keep your map dry by putting it inside a Ziplock bag or a waterproof map case. Then keep it buttoned inside your shirt pocket, or zipped inside a pack which is tied to the canoe. You don't want to lose the map if you turn over!

Careful navigating is worth the extra trouble. It can save you from paddling many extra miles. Even on a bright, sunny day, it's no fun being lost.

To navigate across a lake, look for objects you can steer toward, like trees in the water, or plot your course with the help of shoreline features such as a creek or ridge.

PORTAGES

Portages are places where you have to carry your canoe and gear across land. You may have to portage because of a waterfall, some rapids, or to get from the end of one lake to the beginning of the next. The best portage paths will already be marked on your map. It is much better to follow the path — even when it winds and twists — than to try and make up your own.

When you come to a portage, pull the canoe up beside the bank. Unload all the gear. Now you are ready for the hard part.

One method used by extremely strong people is to have one person carry the canoe upside down over the path. The other person carries the gear.

In the four-man carry, two people grasp the canoe at the thwarts or gunwales on each side.

For people who aren't in training as weight lifters, the best method is the four-man carry. Two people grasp the gunwales or thwarts at the stern, and two at the bow. Carry the canoe right-side up for a distance of about a quarter-mile, or about five football fields. Then set it down. Hike back and pick up the gear. Carry the gear as far as the canoe. Make as many trips as you need to. Then repeat the whole procedure. This method works well unless the trail is overgrown. In that case, turn the canoe upside down and carry it on your shoulders.

When you reach the end of the portage, launch the canoe carefully. Load your gear again. Remember to load the canoe so that it rides slightly higher in the front and does not rock from side to side.

One tip: for a more enjoyable trip, allow yourself plenty of time at each portage. Portaging is hard work. Plan time to snack, swim or nap!

Riffles are places where shallow water rushes over rocks.

CHAPTER SIX

There's music in the sound of running water. The quiet lapping of a pool, the cheerful rushing of a stream over a gravel bar and the powerful crashing of heavy whitewater all have their own magic.

There's also magic in the sight of running water. Water — trickling, dancing, rushing off to somewhere — calls irresistibly to most canoeists.

Listen and look while you paddle. The sights and sounds of the river are not only beautiful. They tell you about the waters you float.

RIFFLES, POOLS AND RAPIDS

"Still water runs deep," is an old saying. It's true. Quiet pools are places where the water is deep.

Shallow water is just the opposite. It runs along quite noisily. You will generally hear a riffle (a place where shallow water rushes over small rocks) before you get there.

Rapids roar from the force of a large amount of water tumbling over boulders. Photo courtesy of The Blue Hole Canoe Company.

Rapids are even noisier than riffles. They roar from the force of a large amount of water tumbling over rocks and boulders. In heavy rapids the surface of the water is almost all white. This is called whitewater. A rapids is sometimes also called a "rock garden."

CURRENTS

Some of the water in a stream flows faster than the rest. Usually, the water near the surface in the middle moves the fastest. Usually, the current flows parallel to the banks of the river. Usually, canoeists ride the main current down a stream. There are exceptions.

SHARP CURVES

In a sharp curve the water does not flow parallel to the banks. If you steer around the curve as you would steer your bicycle, you'll be surprised where you end up. The water will sweep you sideways.

On a sharp curve, stay to the slower side of the channel. Keep the back end of the boat close to the shore on that side, and let the current swing the front end around. Watch for "strainers" which often lie below a sharp curve.

STRAINERS

Strainers are objects in the middle of the current that the water can pass through, but you can't. A fallen tree whose limbs hang down in the water is the most common strainer.

Strainers are extremely dangerous because you can get pinned against them. They break boats and drown people. Strainers are so hazardous because the full force of the water presses against the obstacle. Avoid strainers!

In higher water this fallen sycamore tree would be a very dangerous strainer.

PILLOWS AND IRREGULAR STANDING WAVES

Water is pushed over or around solid obstacles in the stream. A hump in the water means an object lies just beneath the surface. This hump is called a pillow. In a popular stream, the rocks which cause pillows often have silver streaks on them. These silver streaks are from all the aluminum canoes that didn't notice the pillow!

Be suspicious of a lone splashy wave in calm water, or of a standing wave that is higher and splashier than the others nearby. Irregular waves like these mean an object is close by — though not necessarily right underneath the wave.

Look carefully to spot the object submerged in the water. The further downstream the wave is from the object, the deeper the water is going over it. If the wave is several feet away, you are less likely to drag on the object.

DOWNSTREAM "V"s

When more than one object lies in the current, a downstream "V" appears in the water. The "V" will be slick- or glassy-looking compared with the water around it. Usually you should aim right for the "V" and follow the main current. The only time it isn't a good idea to follow the "V" is if you see rocks, pillows, a brush pile, or something similar at the end of the "V."

A downstream "V" marks the deepest part of the channel and you should usually aim right for it.

The waves in the center of this picture are scalloped and even. These haystacks **indicate the water is slowing down, and they would be a fun ride. Photo courtesy of The Blue Hole Canoe Company.**

HAYSTACKS

Haystacks are a series of evenly spaced waves which occur in a group of six or more. Haystacks are not caused by underwater objects, just by the water slowing down as it gets deeper. Haystacks look scalloped and even. They mark the deepest water of the channel and will give you a fun ride.

The water in the left side of the picture flows sideways into an eddy, and then flows slightly upstream.

EDDIES

An eddy is a current which isn't moving downstream. Eddies may even flow upstream a little. They are found behind large rocks in the middle of a stream, or behind other solid objects jutting out from the bank. An eddy is a good place to fish, or to stop and get a drink. In whitewater canoeing, eddies are especially important because they give the canoeist a place to stop and get ready for the next difficult stretch.

YELLOW LIGHT CONDITIONS

Some situations on a river call for caution. For example, what if you have a choice of two narrow, rushing channels that both twist out of sight? On a slow-moving river, try the deepest-looking channel. If you haven't heard any hollering from other canoeists, the channel is probably open. This is on a slow river. On a fast river, or one known to have rapids, be careful! Beach your canoe and go look on foot. Blind passageways can end in a waterfall, a strainer, or a rock garden. Take similar care with long, hidden bends. **When in doubt, get out and scout.**

High water is another situation that calls for caution; it can greatly increase the difficulty of a river. Ask a park ranger or a local outfitter about the water conditions before you put in.

RED LIGHT CONDITIONS

In some conditions it's best to get off the river. One sign of trouble is loudly roaring water. When you hear water crashing, paddle near the bank at once. Don't try to scout from the middle of the stream. When you get close enough to see what's causing the noise, go ashore and take a better look before trying to run the object. Dams, waterfalls, rapids and low-water bridges can all be very dangerous.

Another sure sign of trouble is rapidly rising water. Get off the river and drag your boat up high! Streams can rise ten feet or more under the right conditions. In high water, big trees will go floating down a little creek like Tinker Toys! It's much better to walk, or wait a day, than to tangle with a river in flood stage.

CHAPTER SEVEN

Whitewater! The thrill of it all! Just watching a good whitewater run is exciting. To be able to climb huge waves, grab each eddy, and brace with such skill that you and your boat are one is — terrific, fantastic, incredible!

Whitewater offers a special challenge for those with a keen mind and swift reflexes. Before you become a whitewater champ, you **must** get the proper training and equipment.

TRAINING

Whitewater canoeing is not a sport you can learn on your own. Some of the techniques used to get a canoe through heavy water are the **opposite** of those used on gently flowing streams. In waves four feet high, with giant rocks all around, a bad mistake can be your last mistake.

Get proper instruction. Whitewater clubs often hold special classes and clinics for beginners. An adult with a good whitewater background

These canoeists on the Big Bend Section of the Rio Grande River are following proper safety rules. Members of the party have helped scout these rapids before running them. Photo courtesy of The Blue Hole Canoe Company.

can also teach you. The best way to find a qualified adult is to contact the nearest whitewater club. Ask at a sporting goods store to find out about clubs, or write the American Whitewater Affiliation for a list.

White water canoeing is not a sport you can learn on your own. Join a whitewater club or find a qualified adult to teach you. Photo courtesy of The Blue Hole Canoe Company.

EQUIPMENT

Besides special instruction, you need some special equipment to take on the frothy stuff. To start with, you need a life jacket with an extra amount of lift since whitewater is less buoyant than normal water. A suitable life jacket should also have a zipper and a waist belt.

Next, you need a safety helmet and possibly a wetsuit. The safety helmet will help protect your head, and the wetsuit will insulate your body from the cold water.

You will probably want to get a decked canoe or kayak too. These boats are designed for whitewater, and they are very fast and maneuverable. The exact model for you will depend on whether you intend to race, do some camping or shoot the rapids with a friend. Ask club members and sporting goods stores to tell you about the advantages and disadvantages of each model.

As for paddles, you will probably want to use a double-bladed kayak paddle. Make sure you get one that feels comfortable. Kayak paddles come with either right-handed or left-handed control. Paddles designed just for racing are also available.

RACES

About 500 whitewater and other canoeing races are held each year. Some are mostly for fun and open to everyone. Others are open only to experienced canoeists with special equipment. You can find out about these events by joining one of the organizations mentioned on page nine, by joining a local canoe club or by looking for announcements at sporting goods stores.

Even if you can't enter a race, you will have a great time attending. Canoe races are rarely dull and whitewater races are often spectacular!

CHAPTER EIGHT

Some of the best whitewater racers in the nation own two or three canoes. Why? They expect to bend, puncture and crumple one up every now and then. Things happen — even to the pros.

Things can happen to you too. Suppose you stayed up late last night roasting marshmallows and singing sea chanteys. You're tired. Accidentally, you drop your paddle in the water — right as you enter a swiftly twisting "S" turn. Or, fog rolls in and you can't see far enough to count your toes. Or, you find out your partner is the kind who turns the bathtub over at home.

Suddenly, you've got trouble!

That's why you should travel with at least two other canoes. You may need help or you may have to help someone else in trouble.

The following guide covers some basic situations. In any situation, keep calm. Use common sense. Think! Wear your life jacket **all** the time.

If you capsize in a rapids, **stay upstream from the canoe.** Either hang onto the upstream end and follow the boat through the rapids, or get out of the water and onto a rock.

More importantly, don't get yourself into these situations! **Never** put in on a frothy whitewater stretch without an experienced adult along. **Never** shoot a rapids without looking it over on foot. **Don't** tackle whitewater without the proper safety equipment. As the saying goes, "A bold canoeist doesn't usually become an old canoeist."

YOU RUN AGROUND ON A ROCK

When one end of the canoe runs up on a rock, stay calm. Try backpaddling. This works most of the time. If it doesn't help and the water is too deep to get out, the person whose end is grounded should crawl to the middle of the canoe. This will lighten the boat and let the canoe float free.

The situation is often worse when a rock catches under the middle of the canoe. Rock the canoe gently. Don't rock violently: a jagged rock could pierce the hull. Next, try backpaddling, sidepaddling, or poling with the paddle. Finally, one person may have to crawl to the other end of the canoe or get out. Try not to tip the boat over while you do this.

Slalom racers on the St. Francis River in Missouri pick their way through a rock garden while a large crowd looks on.

YOU ARE SWEPT BACKWARD DOWN A RIFFLE

A riffle is a section of a stream where the water runs fast and shallow. Small rocks usually stick out of the water.

Once you get turned around in a riffle, keep on going backward. The current will take you where the water is deepest. Use your paddle like a pole to keep away from rocks if you have to. Even if you do hit a rock going backward, you will probably just run aground at the stern.

On the other hand, if you try to turn around in midstream, you will likely get broadside to the current and crunch the canoe up on several rocks. You might also turn over.

YOU ARE SWEPT BACKWARD DOWN A RAPIDS

Let's get this straight. Canoeing is a lot of fun, but in some situations it's very dangerous. People drown every year, many times because they get themselves in a bad situation in which there is no good solution.

Once you are in a rapids going backward, sideward or any direction out of control, it is almost too late for advice. The only thing you can do is get to an eddy and stay put until a rescue party can reach you or show you what to do next.

YOU GET TURNED BROADSIDE AGAINST A TREE
OR OTHER OBSTACLE

This is another **very** dangerous situation. It's a good way to drown. Try to avoid the situation to start with! Stay away from sharp turns with trees jutting into the current. Stay away from trees that overhang the river with barely enough space to go underneath them in a canoe. Stay away from any large obstacle in the current. Don't hang onto tree limbs if you do go under a tree!

Suppose, though, you come around a curve and suddenly you see a tree across the stream almost from side to side. In a few seconds you are

If you lean upstream when you are broadside against an obstacle, water will rush into the canoe. This can be another dangerous situation.

broadside too — caught right next to the tree.

Whatever you do, **don't lean upstream.** Lean toward the tree. This sounds wrong. It feels wrong. It feels as though you will tip over and fall out. Of course, you don't want to lean into the tree so far that you do. The worst possible thing would be to get pinned between the canoe and the tree. You don't want to lean upstream either. Water will rush inside your canoe. Then you will probably have a busted canoe.

Lean into the tree and get balanced. Then work together to pull the canoe forward or backward along the obstacle. You may be able to get out of the current this way, or you may be able to get the heavier end to swing downstream.

Be careful. In this situation, if you feel the canoe capsizing anyway, get away from the canoe! You might be pinned between the canoe and the tree, or pressed against the upstream side of the canoe. If possible, get adult help.

YOU TURN OVER ON A RIVER

Unless you capsize right next to an obstacle, try to hang onto your canoe. Grab the upstream end of the boat and swim or walk your canoe to shallow water. Don't hang onto the downstream end because you don't want to get pinned against anything. Hang onto your paddle. Next,

YOU TURN OVER ON A LAKE

Do not try to swim to shore if you turn over on a lake. Stay with your boat. Grab hold of it at once. A small breeze can quickly take it out of reach.

Next, right the canoe if it hasn't already righted itself. It may be full of water, but modern canoes are designed to float even with a heavy load of water inside. Climb in and sit down. Bail out some of the water. If you have several people or a heavily-loaded canoe, you may have to cling to the outside without climbing in. In cold water do your best to get in the canoe and empty it.

After that, head for shore. Use your hands to paddle with if you don't have anything else. Again, try to skip this situation. Check the weather forecast before you go, and seek shelter if you see a storm approaching.

DEEP-WATER CANOE RESCUE

In the event of a capsize, you will be much better off if you have at least three canoes in your party. Two other canoes can rescue a third using the following method.

First, the people in the water should right their canoe and push it between the two rescue canoes. The canoes form the letter "H."

Next, the canoeists in the water should roll the canoe on its side and push down hard on one end. This will make the other end of the canoe come out of the water. The people in one rescue boat can then grab the end of the half-sunken canoe and pull it across their boat.

As the water runs out, the people in the second rescue boat lift the other end out of the water. When the water is all out, the rescuers flip the canoe and slide it back out.

Finally, the capsized canoeists should climb back in while their canoe is steadied by the rescuers. If possible, they should change into dry clothes. Wet clothing can lead to hypothermia.

HYPOTHERMIA

Hypothermia occurs when a person's body loses heat too fast. First victims begin to shiver and feel numb. Then they start acting very tired or as though they can't think. When the weather is cold, or a person is wet, it is possible to die from this condition in just a few hours. In the old days, when people said someone "died from exposure," they meant that someone had died of hypothermia.

If one of your companions on a canoe trip seems to be chilled to the bone and is acting like a zombie, stop at once. Put the victim in his or her underwear inside a sleeping bag or under a pile of coats. Have another person in his or her underwear get in too. Don't worry about what people think. You may be saving someone's life.

Get adult help right away. Also heat some soup — or even hot water — for the victim to drink. Quick first aid is the only thing that will save a person who has hypothermia.

Canoeing can be rough. Sometimes you get baked in the sun and drenched in the rain. After three hours in wet tennis shoes, your feet look like wrinkled prunes. Your back starts aching, your rump gets flat, and maybe you wind up swimming in spring-fed water.

Who would do such a thing and call it fun?

How can you explain that your spine tingles when you set off in the swirling mist with a fresh breeze and a fat lunch? What words describe the thrill of watching blue herons swoop low over deep green water? Why does your heart go thump, thump, thump when you first hear the roar of whitewater around the bend?

An old song from the northern lakes tells how some people feel about journeys in a canoe:

> "Swift as the silver fish,
> Canoe of birch bark,
> O'er mighty waterways
> Carries me far.
> Blue lake and rocky shore,
> I will return once more . . ."

If you have never been canoeing, you may wonder why this song ends with the words "I will return once more." If you have been canoeing, you know why. Canoeing seeps into your bones, your blood, your inner self. You always want to go "one more time."

Life on the waterway is a great life!